I0310450

Praise for *Opportunity Cost*

"*Opportunity Cost* is a skillfully built sequence about grappling with the aftermath of assault. Ordinarily innocuous parts of language, like punctuation and the act of editing ones words, become powerful tools with which the poet explores the torturous ways we negotiate pain caused by those close to us. It is a unique book on an often difficult to navigate topic. I am grateful for it, grateful to the poet who crafted it."

Kazim Ali, Guest Judge, author of *The Voice of Sheila Chandra*

"This book is awake to its own pain. This book is determined to put it on the record. For me, this book is true solace, stark truth—therefore necessary for all of us to read."

Alessandra Lynch, author of *Pretty Tripwire*

"*Opportunity Cost* is a stunning collection of poems that orbit a luminous and relentless rage, but also cling tight to a relationship with survival, with pleasure, with everything on the other side. And it is that, that reaching towards an understanding of an after that allows these poems to sing well beyond the page."

Hanif Abdurraqib, author of *A Fortune for Your Disaster*

"The poems in Abby Johnson's *Opportunity Cost* show us how assault changes the way a person experiences the world. Everything becomes a reminder, a threat: the movers who steal underwear off her dresser, the rain which touches the speaker without her consent, even—or perhaps, especially—language. In the poem "He," the assailant infects every single word. In the series, "To My Assailant's Wife," the speaker struggles between what to reveal and what to erase. Who can the speaker trust with her story? Can she trust you?"

Paige Lewis, author of *Space Struck*

Opportunity Cost

poems by Abby Johnson

Published in the United States of America by Frontier Poetry
www.frontierpoetry.com

ISBN 978-0-578-29948-8

Cover artwork by Scoot Swain.
Book and cover design by Julianne Johnson.

Opportunity Cost:

When one person makes a choice
and a potential world vanishes

Contents

Opportunity Cost

If: he assaults me

then: strip to shame: shower twice a day

If: taste the word: whisper it: slut

then: whimper prayer: let this: be pure

If: pucker at sting of lemon: cut open: another

then: wail when it storms: no one listens

If: panic is a body

then: it marries: me

If: he does not assault me

then: my name spoken: my own voice

If: desire is clear water: sand at the bottom

then: mirror: image

If: breathing slowly like a child

then: alone with a man: comfort

If: unimaginable if: I want it

then: I want it

To My Assailant's Wife

~~You are so pretty~~ you ~~must~~ deserve to be treated well.

It seems cruel to tell you this now.

Afterward

He is licking, like
he reached
the greasy cardboard
bottom of the wing bucket,
finger by finger,
deliberately. So,
I burn the dress.

I See My Assailant's Mother Everywhere

buying radishes in the grocery store,
renting a car, pushing a stroller
with a newborn baby girl in it, ordering
a doppio over ice with heavy

whipping cream. She lived with grief,
as though with child. The spirit removed
from her bloated body by flash flood.
The car was found first and then

the simple, soft bob of brown
hair, and then the body
resting against the river rocks.
I shouldn't tell this story, but I know

grief achieves equilibrium
like particles of water,
or death, moving down
until most and least mean

nothing. Like water sweeping down
the road toward where there is no water,
I am flooded by the diffusion of pain,
haunted by visions, unearned grief,

and a stolen sorrow which sounds like *O, god*
of water, grant him rest for this one regret.
She went to the river knowing
nothing of where his hands had been.

To My Assailant's Pregnant Sister

My hornet-nest torso buzzed and quivered
when you hugged me. Your belly pulsed humanoid
and brief, a swift kick and then nothing.
If your child is a boy like your brother,
he will have hands insistent
to touch. You cried into my shoulder.
The boy in your belly pushed
one ear to the wall of his shaky house
to hear my hornets. Heredity tells me
he will look like my assailant, but redder
and rawer. I am afraid you will love
the resemblance. I am afraid I will hold him
and look into an innocent face.
Before you pull away the small boy stretches
his handprint into your skin,
touching me at the waist.
I flinch. You don't
notice. You say you can't wait
for me to meet him.

A Mouth Opening

against yours is a wound
that will not heal, the minister said.
Watch this video of a hawk
with a field mouse in its beak.
You don't want to be eaten,
do you?

Well, do you?
And then the girls in school came
to class with rings from their fathers,
the pledge of prey, each silver band
reflecting moonstone white
like an exposed bone.

Like an exposed bone,
he showed it to me: the scar
above his knuckle. *My mother gave it to me,*
he said. *I called her a bitch and, when she ducked,*
my hand slipped into the drywall
and I left a mark.

And I left. A mark
of some lesser message: not, he wanted
to hit her and missed. He wanted to touch her
and reached. He reached for me and I did not duck.
The cloth center of the bandaid
stained like a rag. I am

stained like a rag. *I am*
telling you this to keep you
safe, he said. *Every vulture loves the body*
it circles and picks to keep the bones
clean. You want to be loved someday,
don't you?

Don't you
know what they do to the bandage
once it's unbound? You might as well let me
keep touching you. The hawk cradles
the field mouse in its maw until
the mouth clamps shut.

The mouth clamps shut
against mine. Hard and rough,
I pull it closer. I want it to want me.
I am afraid of dying. He keeps saying,
you will never have this again, until I am
only a mouth opening.

To My Assailant's Wife

~~His fingers happened to me. His rancid breath in my ear happened to me.~~ I hope it's different for you. ~~I hate that it's different for you.~~

Blueberry Picking

Through the greenhouse roof, it sprinkles
and I think all precipitation is the weather touching me
without my consent. Earlier at brunch, before
blueberry picking, my childhood friends say *thank god*
none of us have ever been raped. Have you ever stood
on a roof and looked down? It does not feel
as much like flying as you imagine. I have stains
all down the lap of my dress and across my lips.
The owner says we are the last customers of the season,
that when the doors close behind us, they will stay closed
until spring. I tell my friends we should come back
next summer, but I can still taste the insecticide
and we have four bags bursting with overripe berries.
The rain keeps tapping my shoulders, and I wish
I were looking down from the roof of a skyscraper.

He

after Nicole Sealey

The hero: a preacher's heir
and hedonist, schemes.
He heard her
shriek, became heartless.
He switched his sheets. The heathen.

The hero's psyche, overheating
heart. He seethes. He inherits heaven, cheats
and wheedles. Apprehended by ache,
he searches. He finishes. His lightheart
sheer with heaven. He finishes.

He, blithe. Her,
cherubic. Then, cheek
to sheet, he pushed, he sheared
then breached. Or heaved
then finished. Whichever.

The Assailant's Mother On My Television Sends Me a Message

After Robin Coste Lewis

"I just can't surrender to this notion that he was evil."

Just surrender. I notion he can't. This was evil.

Evil just can't surrender. This he was.

This was just. Surrender to that notion.

That notion was evil. This he can't surrender.

Can't this evil surrender.

To this evil he was notion.

To this evil, was I just?

I was evil.

I can't surrender.

Evil just can't surrender I.

To he, I was.

To I, he was I.

Surrender this notion to he.

Surrender I.

He was evil. I surrender

Afterward

He is

He is licking

He is licking, like he

He is licking, like he reached

He is licking, like he reached the greasy

He is licking, like he reached the greasy cardboard

He is licking, like he reached the greasy cardboard bottom

He is licking, like he reached the greasy cardboard bottom of the wing

He is licking, like he reached the greasy cardboard bottom of the wing bucket,

He is licking, like he reached the greasy cardboard bottom of the wing bucket, finger

He is licking, like he reached the greasy cardboard bottom of the wing bucket, finger by finger,

He is licking, like he reached the greasy cardboard bottom of the wing bucket, finger by finger, deliberately.

He is licking, like he reached the greasy cardboard bottom of the wing bucket, finger by finger, deliberately. So, I burn

He is licking, like he reached the greasy cardboard bottom of the wing bucket, finger by finger, deliberately. So, I burn the dress.

To My Assailant's Wife

Tell me what you see in him. ~~I usually float~~
~~above my body when someone mentions~~
~~his name, but~~ I want to hear what you have
to say. I imagine you will say something like:

He is kind.

> ~~He stopped touching me~~
> ~~fifteen minutes after I told him to.~~

He is thoughtful.

> ~~He pointed out every thing he loved~~
> ~~about the girls walking in front of us.~~

He has a good sense of humor.

> ~~When he left I laughed~~
> ~~with relief.~~

It Happened Once in a Dream

Every night *(I dream)* I am buried
under forest. *(I push)* through fertile dirt,

beholden to *(the man)* who put me there.
I sprout through dirt *(into)* crackling night air,

wet with mud and *(water)* that sustains roots,
I crouch, afraid *(and when)* the woods appear

calm, suddenly *(I hear)* a heavy cry
I recognize *(his howls)* and run, deeper

into the woods. *(I do)* not hear footsteps
but fear I will *(not reach)* open air alone.

As I run, I stretch *(out my)* arm into white light
and now, I see my *(own hand)* looks sinister.

Inventory of Lost Things

I. She says, *I want to see if I'm normal,*
show me yours. I flash my popsicle purple
tongue. *I meant let's both take off*
our swimsuits, just to see. I say *I don't want to.*
She says *we'll turn off the lights*. We do,
and see nothing, and never tell.

II. The teacher said, *see this gum,*
I put it in my mouth
already. Do you want
to put it in your mouth?
This is you. This is you:
Disgusting.

III. His hand on my inner thigh again, it moves
up, he makes his fingers disappear.
A chaperone sees it happen.
I hurry to my hotel room, find her
waiting for me, one dim light on.
She prophesies: *He hurts girls*
like you. You should know
better than to let him.

IV. After doing laundry at my mother's house,
she says: *I left your peach silk underwear*
on the dresser when some men moved in my new mattress
and now they're gone. Like a party trick, a sleight
of hand. I have lost more artifacts than I can pray to. And more
go missing, slipping into pockets, carried off. Still, my body,
obstinate, leaves traces of itself, a sheen
of shame, a glistening.

To My Assailant's Wife

I have never met you, ~~but I dream of you~~
~~on your wedding day, glimmering and wrapped~~
~~in white tulle like morning light.~~
~~I stand at the back of the sanctuary,~~
~~a filthy mass of damp dirt, roughly shaped,~~
~~into a facsimile of the bride,~~ but I still hope
your day is perfect.

Opportunity Cost

"the loss of potential gain from other alternatives when someone makes a choice."

want	panic
the unimaginable	wail in a storm
comfort alone with a man	sting like lemon
to breath slowly like a child	whimpered prayer
clear water	*slut*
my name spoken	shame shower
no assault	assault

To My Assailant's Wife

You have no reason to believe me, ~~but I can show you the message where he admits to what he did. He sent his apologies through instagram direct message while I was asleep. I can send you screenshots. I checked your instagram for a year for any hint, but I don't think you know~~ and I don't want you to know who I am.

On the Day My Assailant Gets Engaged

my boyfriend calls me lovely
and my breath escapes
like a bad spirit from the body
of a pig. My arms go flaccid
as a worm corpse. I twist the sheet
around my wedding finger
and preen.

Acknowledgements

"I See My Assailant's Mother Everywhere:" was first published in *Sycamore Review* (Volume 30 Issue 2).

"To My Assailant's Pregnant Sister" was first published in *Sycamore Review* (Volume 30 Issue 2).

"He" is after Nicole Sealey's poem titled "And."

"The Assailant's Mother on my Television Sends Me a Message" is after Robin Coste Lewis' poem titled "verga:." The quoted line is delivered by Meryl Streep's character on the show *Big Little Lies*.

Abby Johnson is a poet and a Hoosier who is proud of the local art scene that fostered her. She received her MFA in Creative Writing through Butler University. During her time there, she served as Poetry Co-Editor for *Booth: A Journal*. She has poems published in *Turnpike Magazine*, *Josephine Quarterly*, *The Indianapolis Review*, and most recently in the Winter/Spring 2020 issue of *Sycamore Review*.

www.ingramcontent.com/pod-product-compliance
Lightning Source LLC
Chambersburg PA
CBHW072023290426
44109CB00018B/2326
* 9 7 8 0 5 7 8 2 9 9 4 8 8 *